Abigail

BECOMING A WOMAN
OF UNDERSTANDING

YONNIE FOWLER

WESTBOW
PRESS®
A DIVISION OF THOMAS NELSON
& ZONDERVAN

WestBow Press books may be ordered through booksellers or by contacting:

WestBow Press
A Division of Thomas Nelson & Zondervan
1663 Liberty Drive
Bloomington, IN 47403
www.westbowpress.com
1 (866) 928-1240

ISBN: 978-1-5127-9771-8 (sc)
ISBN: 978-1-5127-9770-1 (e)

Library of Congress Control Number: 2017911922

Print information available on the last page.

WestBow Press rev. date: 07/31/2017

To God and to my Lord and Savior Jesus the Christ. I thank my beloved companion, God's precious Holy Spirit, for inspiration and guidance throughout the writing of this book and beforehand as He shared with me 2 Peter 1:5–7, my guideline for spiritual growth.

Contents

Acknowledgments

I would like to thank my husband, Billy R. Fowler, and my family for encouraging me to write this book. To the women of Second Missionary Baptist Church of Jackson, Michigan, I would like to thank you for diligently attending the numerous Bible study classes where you allowed me to pour out my thoughts on this subject. To Covington Theological Seminary, I thank you for preparing me to push toward this goal.

Introduction

In 1 Samuel 25 (KJV), Abigail is noted as being a woman of good understanding. She is referred to as "Abigail the Carmelitees, Nabal's widow" (1 Samuel 27:3 NKJV). Abigail's husband, Nabal, was a wealthy sheep master. Nabal was a hot-tempered, drunken man who was rude and evil in his doings, and he was so mean that no one could reason with him. When David was hiding from the jealous King Saul, he sent ten men to Nabal for food for himself and his men. Nabal blatantly refused. David, who had protected people in the area from bands of robbers, was so angered by Nabal's refusal that he had determined to kill Nabal and every male in his household.

Abigail realized the danger threatening her family because of Nabal's stupidity; in her wisdom, she gathered enough food for David's men. Taking two hundred loaves of bread, two bottles of wine, five sheep already dressed, one and a half bushels of roasted grain, one hundred clusters of raisins, and two hundred cakes of figs, she loaded them on donkeys and rode out to meet David. Bowing before him to show her respect, she apologized for her husband's behavior. By quickly agreeing with David that Nabal had acted with great disrespect, she soothed David's anger.

When Abigail returned home, she found a great feast in progress. Oblivious to his narrow brush with death, Nabal's heart was merry, for he was very drunk. Abigail waited until the next morning to tell him of the destruction and death that he almost brought upon his household. Nabal's "heart died within him, and he became like a stone" (1 Samuel 25:37 NKJV). Nabal died ten days later, apparently from the shock of discovering his near brush with death.

When David heard that Nabal was dead, he proposed to Abigail. Abigail's understanding saved her family, and it caught the heart of David so that he provided her with his love and protection. She later became one of his wives.

> Let not the wise man boast of his wisdom, neither let not the mighty man boast in his might, let not the rich man boast in his riches; but let him who boast, boast of this, that he understands and knows Me. (Jeremiah 9:23–24 ESV)

CHAPTER 1

Understanding Faith

One night, God revealed to me in a dream seven steps that I would need for my spiritual walk with Christ. I was awakened after each step, although at the time, I had not grown enough in my walk with the Lord to know that I should always keep a pencil and a pad of paper on my nightstand to write down thoughts that God shares with me throughout the night. When I awoke in the morning, I remembered the dream but not the important details that were to be written down and used for my spiritual growth. God, in His kindness and mercy and knowing my frailty, showed me in the Bible a year later the seven steps that He had revealed to me that night in the dream. To the woman seeking understanding through spiritual growth, I share these seven steps with you.

> Giving all diligence, add to your faith, virtue [goodness], and to goodness knowledge, and to knowledge self-control, and to self-control perseverance [patience], and to patience godliness [devotion to God], and to devotion to God brotherly kindness [concern for others],

and to concern for others charity [love]. (2 Peter
1:5–7 KJV)

For if you do these things you will never stumble.
(2 Peter 1:10 NKJV)

God desires that we be spiritually grounded, steadfast, and
unmovable. God wants us to stand firm in our faith in Him, and
He does not want us to be tossed back and forth or blown here and
there. Instead, He wants us to be rooted and grounded in Him as
partakers of His divine nature.

Now faith is the substance of things hoped for, the
evidence of things not seen. (Hebrews 11:1 KJV)

Through my faith in God, I knew Him as my Savior. God now
wanted me to trust Him to be my Lord. I knew that, if I died, I
would go to heaven. God wanted me to trust Him here on earth
with my everyday situations.

Faith comes by hearing, and hearing by the word
of God. (Romans 10:17 NKJV)

I purchased a Good News Bible to foster my understanding. I
began to faithfully study the Word of God, comparing the King
James Bible with the Good News Bible. The Lord began revealing
Himself to me, and I began to trust God when situations looked
bleak and when I had no answers.

In Proverbs 3:5–6, I learned that if I would trust in the Lord
with all my heart, and not depend on my own understanding, if I
would acknowledge God in all my ways, He would direct my path.
Studying God's Word became exciting. God began showing me
truth after truth in His Word. He also allowed circumstances into
my life to prove to me that His Word is true. I read in His Word

that He is a healer, and God proved to me that He heals. I read that He would work things out for my good, and God proved to me that He is faithful. I read that He was a burden bearer, and God proved that He is my comforter. Time after time, God showed Himself to be faithful. God's Word became perpetually real to me.

In 1 Samuel 25, I read about a woman named Abigail who was noted for being a woman of good understanding. She was intelligent and sympathetic, and she possessed the ability to settle differences with mutual agreements. Her wisdom was shown through her faith in God. He keeps covenant and mercy with those who love Him and keep His commandments. Her faith was demonstrated through her love for God and for her neighbor.

Faith without works is dead. (James 2:20 KJV)

Abigail's faith was demonstrated through her marriage to Nabal. Nabal was a very wealthy man. The Bible says that his possessions were in Carmel: three thousand sheep, and one thousand goats. He was wealthy, but he was also full of pride and arrogance. He used his influence of wealth and power to control those subject to his authority. In fact, Nabal's very name meant fool.

The story of Abigail took place during the time when jealous King Saul was seeking to kill David. David was hiding in the wilderness of Paran, where Nabal's shepherds were tending the sheep. While David and his men were in the wilderness, they became as a wall to Nabal's shepherds. David's men were protection for the shepherds—not hurting them or taking anything from them.

In the wilderness of Paran, David received word that it was sheep-shearing time for Nabal. Sheep shearing is a time of festivity, with food and drinks. David knew that Nabal was wealthy and would have more than enough to share. Since his men had shown so much kindness toward Nabal's shepherds, David thought Nabal would not mind sharing out of his abundance. But rather than returning the kindness, Nabal railed at David.

> One of Nabal's young men told Abigail to consider what she must do; for there was certain to be trouble for her and her family. The young man said that Nabal was such a scoundrel that a man could not speak to him. (1 Samuel 25:14–17)

After hearing this news, Abigail ran to God, seeking His direction for how to deal with her foolish husband. Significantly, she ran to God rather than running to Nabal; a wise woman picks her battles carefully.

Abigail did not spend time fussing with her husband over the imprudent words he had spoken to David. Instead, she got busy doing what was right. Abigail knew that, through faith, she could ask God, and He would come through for her. If we want God to answer our prayers, then that must be our expectation when we pray. Faith moves God!

Romans 12:11 tells us that we are not to be slothful in business while we serve the Lord. Abigail became busy doing that which was right. She trusted God, and He showed her how to do everything that needed to be done.

Abigail hurriedly prepared the best of her substance for David: two hundred loaves of freshly baked bread, two bottles of the best wine, five sheep that had already been slaughtered, one and a half bushels of roasted corn, one hundred clusters of raisins, and two hundred fig cakes. God showed her the way to David's heart.

> If your enemy is hungry, feed him. (Romans 12:20 NKJV)

Abigail could have given half-heartedly, but instead, she chose to give her best. She did just what God does; He gives us His best.

What man is there of you, whom if his son ask
bread, will he give him a stone? Or if he asks a fish,
will he give him a serpent? If you then, being evil,
know how to give good gifts to your children, how
much more shall your Father which is in heaven
give good things to them that ask him? (Matthew
7:9–11 KJV)

Through faith, Abigail trusted God and gave David her best. As
my faith in God began to grow, I came to realize that God desired
for me to come before Him not with a cup but rather with a
bucket. Faith moves God.

But without faith it is impossible to please Him:
for he that comes to God must believe that He is,
and that He is a rewarder of those who diligently
seek Him. (Hebrews 11:6 NKJV)

We must not put limits on our trust in God. God is a big God who
can do above all that we may ask or think. God does not want us
to think small; we must make our thinking big enough for God
to fit in. God wants us to trust Him for great things.

Abigail possessed a confident attitude that God would work
things out for her and for the good of her entire family. Abigail
must have seen God work many times in the past while dealing
with her foolish husband; therefore, she had no reason to doubt
Him. God had always made a way, and if He did it for her before,
He would surely do it again.

David had asked Nabal for food, but he already knew in his
heart that God would supply his need—with or without Nabal's
help.

The Lord is my shepherd, I shall not want. (Psalm
23 KJV)

Nabal did not realize that he was an instrument chosen by God to help David. If he had realized that, he would not have acted so repulsively.

Let us take an inward look at ourselves. How many times have we missed an opportunity to give? Maybe we didn't have a rude attitude as Nabal did—or maybe we simply ignored the opportunity. I remember a time when I ignored a chance to give because I was not bold enough to step up and address the issue at hand. I was in the checkout line at a drugstore during my lunch hour. In front of me, a woman was having a conversation with her small child. I couldn't help overhearing the woman reprimanding her child for taking her wallet out of her purse while playing before they left home. They now had no money to pay for their items or for the bus fare to return home. I had the money to pay for her grocery items and the bus fare, but instead of interjecting to offer assistance, I just stood there with everyone else, ignoring her situation. After I made my purchase, I walked out of the store and looked to see if I could locate the lady, but she was nowhere to be found. That was many years ago, but I still remember it as though it was yesterday. I told myself that I would never let an opportunity to be God's obedient servant pass me by again.

There are times when people are not always truthful or legit, but we have to trust God with all our hearts and lean not unto our own understanding while God directs our paths.

When I have not prayerfully allowed God to direct my path, I end up with blinders on that cause me to miss seeing someone's need. This hurts me. When I allow God to direct my path, I never regret being too kind.

> A good woman will show favor and lend: she will guide her affairs with discretion. (Psalm 112:5)

Wise understanding comes from God—and not us. Abigail's faith in God directed her to do that which was right toward her husband in a respectful way that honored God. She did not team up with her husband in condemning David; she lined up with God and trusted Him whose ways are always right. God will never fail us when we place our trust in Him.

Abigail's faith in God gave her the courage to act humbly rather than displaying an attitude of pride. Humble people focus more on God and others than they do on themselves. True humility does not produce pride. It produces gratitude. When Abigail saw David, she quickly dismounted the donkey and fell with her face to the ground in front of David. In humbling herself before David, Abigail called David Lord and told him to let Nabal's guilt be upon her. To address David, knowing that he was dreadfully angry and was on his way to kill every man in Nabal's household, including Nabal, took courage that only comes from God. For Abigail to ask David to place Nabal's guilt upon her was an act of total submission unto God. For if she lived, she lived unto God, and if she died, she died unto God.

When our total dependence is upon God, we learn as Abigail did, that God will never leave us or forsake us. We learn, without a shadow of a doubt, that we can depend on God. Abigail's total existence was dependent on God giving her courage. If David was determined to kill Nabal, he could have killed her as well.

Physical courage is based on moral courage, a reliance on the presence and power of God, and a commitment to His commandments.

> Have I not commanded you? Be strong and of good courage; be not afraid, neither be dismayed, for the Lord your God is with you wherever you go. (Joshua 1:9 NKJV)

> Behave courageously, and the Lord will be with the good. (2 Chronicles 19:11 KJV)

Abigail was confident that she was doing what God required of her. She knew that if God was for her, who would dare be against her. That was why Abigail could boldly tell David to let Nabal's foolish actions be upon her. She knew that God—whom she served—would fight her battle. Beyond that, Abigail knew that the battle was not hers—it was the Lord's. God tells us to cast all of our cares upon Him because He cares for us. When we give our problems and situations to God, He says that it is not by might, nor by power, but by His Spirit that He will fight for us.

> For we wrestle not against flesh and blood, but against principalities, against powers, against the rulers of the darkness of this world, against spiritual wickedness in high places. (Ephesians 6:12 KJV)

> If you have faith as small a mustard seed, you can say to this mountain, "Move from here to there," and it will move. Nothing will be impossible for you. (Matthew 17:20 NKJV)

Those who have faith the size of a mustard seed are able to speak to their situations. They are able to speak into existence the things that seem as though they are not (Romans 4:17). We speak into existence cursings or blessings, and our lives follows our words. "Death and life are in the power of the tongue" (Proverbs 18:21 KJV).

Abigail approached David and said, "The Lord has kept you from murdering and taking vengeance into your own hands" (1 Samuel 25:26 NLT). When Abigail first approached David, she was uncertain how he would respond to her. Therefore, the words that Abigail spoke to David were spoken in faith. She could have pleaded with David not to kill her family. Instead, she chose by faith to speak blessings into existence. We have the same opportunity to speak blessings into our situations. The Bible says that it only takes faith the size of the smallest seed (a mustard seed).

When we have faith in God, we will do things that no one will understand—sometimes not even ourselves. Faith is all about trusting in the unseen and the unknowing with the assurance that God will work it out. We only know that it is in God that we trust. When our backs are up against a wall and we don't know what else to do, we must trust God. God is the reassurance of our salvation.

Trusting in God, I decided to go on a trip to South Africa by myself. Throughout the two-week trip, God was my constant companion. I observed the beautiful scenery, and I was captivated by the essence of wildlife. My heart wrenched at the downtrodden poverty and the reflections of apartheid.

When the day came for me to return home, I awoke early to make sure I would be among the first to board the bus that would take me to the airport for my long trip home. After eating breakfast, I gathered up my luggage and made my way to the hotel lobby. When I asked where to catch a bus to the airport, I was told that I must sign a sheet stating my destination and the time I would need to arrive.

Being one of the first in line to board the bus when it arrived, I found my thoughts joyfully reflecting over my two weeks in South Africa. It wasn't long before the bus arrived. I placed my luggage in the designated area for the attendant to make sure it was stored in the underneath luggage bend. Choosing a seat by a window, I sat down and thanked the Lord for keeping me safe and being my constant companion throughout the trip. I breathed a sigh of contentment, knowing that my trip had ended and I was on my way home to share my experiences in South Africa.

After people finally filled the bus, the lady in the hotel lobby who had given me the bus instructions approached me. She told me that I would have to get off that bus and get on the next bus. Apparently, everyone on the bus was also headed for the airport, but they needed to get there before I did. Without putting up a fuss, I kindly got off the bus and asked the attendant to remove my luggage, which was at the bottom of the stack. *Lord, you have so diligently kept me during these two weeks. Surely you are in charge of this also.*

When the next bus came along, I handed my luggage to the attendant and boarded the bus. The bus filled up, and we headed to the airport. It wasn't long before it started to drizzle, and then the drizzle turned into a downpour. It was raining so hard that the traffic lights went out, which caused a major traffic jam. All I could hear was honking. The police finally made their way through the jam to direct traffic.

We arrived at the airport three hours later. After getting off the bus and locating our luggage, we found out that our plane had left. There would not be another plane leaving for the United States until the following evening. For quite some time, we all just stood around and looked at each other with blank stares. At that point, a man decided to take charge and be the leader of the group. He got on his phone, talked with someone, and came back to us with the news that we would be having dinner and spending the night in a villa.

By the time we reached the restaurant, the rain had stopped. The dinner was nice, but with the anticipation of not knowing where I would be spending the night, I cannot remember what I ate. I realized that everyone except me had a companion. I knew that God was present with me.

By the time everyone completed dinner, it was dark. There were no streetlights or porch lights; I couldn't even see my hand in front of my face. The only lights were the headlights on the shuttle bus, which had come to pick us up and drop us off at our designated areas for the night. The shuttle bus did not have doors or windows.

It wasn't until we were being dropped off at our designated areas for the night that the reality of the situation really hit me. I was about to be dropped off in the dark—to a villa I couldn't even see. Nonetheless, I said, "Okay, Lord. It's me and you!" When it was my turn to get off the shuttle bus, my eyes had finally become adjusted to the dark. I could see the outline of my villa.

After making my way to the door and opening it, my eyes had to adjust to darkness. I brushed my hand along the wall in search of a light. I finally found it! The window drapes were closed, and I knew there was no need to look out the window because all that I would see at that time would be darkness. The only thing I could think of to do was get ready for bed. I went into the bathroom and searched for a light. I found it and began my nightly routine. It didn't take too long for me to realize that my ears were hearing the outdoors. I reached my hand behind the bathroom curtain and realized that the window was wide open. The outdoors startled me, and I quickly shut the window. I finished in the bathroom and went back into the other room. I noticed another door and opened it. Once again, just like in the bathroom, the only thing I saw beyond the door was darkness. I closed that door too.

Hoping that the evening would soon come to an end, I climbed under the covers and turned off the light. I wasn't about to sleep with the lights on because if someone slipped in while I was sleeping, at least they wouldn't be able to see me right off the bat. Plus, if they couldn't see me when they came in and I saw them, I would have time to pray!

Before drifting off to sleep I prayed: *Thank you, Lord, for keeping me—and may daylight come soon!* During the night, I found myself sleeping on and off. When daybreak finally arrived, I quickly got out of bed and went to the huge picture window in the room where I had been sleeping. I opened the curtain, and to my surprise the window was wide open. Anything or anyone could have walked right in.

God said, "Yonnie, you thought I kept you in South Africa— and I did—but I wanted to show you how I could really keep you!"

No doubt about it—God is a promise keeper! I serve a mighty, faithful God.

God kept me despite my fear. He never changes, and He never wavers. No matter how far we travel or what obstacles we face, God is completely and perfectly faithful forever.

> Therefore know that the Lord your God, He is God, the faithful God who keeps covenant and mercy for a thousand generations with those who love Him and keep His commandments. (Deuteronomy 7:9 NKJV)

No matter what happens in life, we can depend on God.

As a spouse, Abigail was faithful. She was there for her husband—even when he didn't know that he needed her. She faithfully took care of business and was not slothful in executing matters pertaining to life. Through Abigail's trust in God, she showed herself to be faithful to Nabal by being a wife who he could count on.

CHAPTER 2

Understanding Goodness

To my faith, add goodness. Oh, give thanks unto the Lord, for He is good, and not we. If God is good and not ourselves, how do we obtain goodness? Goodness in the perfect state is a word used only to describe God. In Luke 18:18–19 (NKJV), a religious leader addressed Jesus as "Good Teacher." Jesus responded by asking the religious leader, "Why do you call me good?" Jesus went on to tell him that no one is good except God.

> Jesus went about doing good … for God was with Him. (Acts 10:38 KJV)

The source and power of Jesus's goodness is God. If there be any good in us, it is only because God's precious Holy Spirit dwells within us. The more we grow and become like Christ, the more of God we have in us, thus the more goodness we possess.

Abigail understood that the working power of her goodness toward David was God. She knew that being kind to David would overcome the evil that was intended. There is power in goodness to overcome evil. My father used to always say, "Whip them with kindness." We can stand against adversity because God is good.

Be not overcome of evil, but overcome evil with
good. (Romans 12:21 KJV)

I'm reminded of a time in my life when evil was overcome by
kindness. One morning when I was headed downstairs to prepare
breakfast, my husband began to fuss. Rather than fussing back, I
reminded the Lord that my husband was His child. As I continued
downstairs, I put a song in my heart. As I was preparing breakfast,
I actually forgot that he was even fussing upstairs. A short time
later, my husband came downstairs and sat at the kitchen table.
He stated that he wanted to apologize for fussing, and he went on
to tell his story of what he had just experienced. As he was looking
in his closet for what he would wear that day, while still fussing,
a force took his head and rammed it really hard against the side
of the closet door.

I praised the Lord and gave Him thanks for overcoming evil.
God had allowed kindness to overcome evil. God wants us to seek
Him and not revenge. When we seek God, we always find the best.

Amid the evil of this world, God is good. Early one bitter cold
December morning, I was headed to work while it was still dark.
I felt the need to let my car warm up before leaving. I thought I
would just go out, start the car, and come back inside while it
warmed up. I had money in my purse that I had been saving in
an envelope. I never save money in my purse. As I was about to
walk out the door, I felt a need to take the money out of my purse.
I listened to the unction of God's Holy Spirit and decided to leave
my purse in the house.

I walked out the door with only the key to my car in my hand.
Just as I approached the driver's side, I heard a voice from the
street asking if I had a quarter to use the telephone. I knew that
there were no pay telephones in the area, and I became leery. I felt
like I should turn around and go back inside.

Before I could get halfway to the door, the voice said, "Hold
it right there."

I turned around to find myself staring down the barrel of a gun. The thought crossed my mind that it was just like the movies. The man holding the gun was stocky, and I knew from his facial expression that he meant business. He grabbed me and put the gun to my head. I could smell liquor on his breath, and I knew I was not just dealing with a man. He instructed me to walk to the door. I followed his instructions, but before I reached the door, I grabbed a pillar.

I knew in my spirit that this man was going to have to kill me right there. I was not going to allow him to pry me from the pillar and take me away where no one would be able to find me. As I held on tightly to the pillar, I told the man that Jesus loves him. He totally disregarded my words and continued to pry my hands loose, insisting that I move away from the door.

At that point, I saw my life flash before me. I knew that if I died, I would go to be with the Lord. I began to think of my children and how I wanted to raise them up in the fear and admonition of the Lord. I wanted to live. The door to the house opened, and my heart sprung with hope. Right away, the door closed. Just as quickly as hope had appeared, it seemed to have vanished.

Hope does not disappoint. (Romans 5:5 NKJV)

The man began to run as fast as his legs could carry him. I have never had so many emotions flood my being at one time. With one swift movement, my hand opened the door. With the next movement, my shaking legs were swiftly swept inside. God will make our enemies flee and become confused (Deuteronomy 28:7).

I had to go to court to testify, and I found out that he began to run because he thought someone was after him. In fact, he was so sure that someone was after him that he stole someone's car in order to get away. They owner of the stolen car called the police. After searching the area, the police spotted the vehicle. After a wild chase, the man ended up being cornered. He jumped out of the stolen car and began running.

The police finally captured the man, and when they tried to put handcuffs on him, the handcuffs barely fit his wrists.

> Be not overcome of evil, but overcome evil with good. (Romans 12:21 KJV)

With a gun to my head, I said, "Jesus loves you." I knew that goodness was dependent upon God. And because God is so good, He made my enemy flee and become confused. He's that good!

> Great is the Lord and He is greatly to be praised. (Psalm 48:1 KJV)

God explained to us what is good. The Lord requires us to do what is right, to love tenderly, and to walk humbly with our God (Micah 6:8).

> Keep your heart with all diligence, for out of it spring the issues of life. (Proverbs 4:23 NKJV)

Pure water can flow only from a pure spring; likewise, goodness can only flow from an honest and good heart. Guard your heart so that you will not be overcome of evil. With an honest and good heart you will overcome evil with good.

> Do men gather grapes from thorn bushes or figs from thistles? (Matthew 7:16–17 NKJV)

Just as good fruit comes from a good tree, people are known by the fruit they bear. Good fruit is the yield of a good tree, and goodness is the product of a good person. The test of good people is the fruit they bear.

> The fruit of the Spirit is: Love, joy, peace, long-suffering, gentleness, goodness, and faith. (Galatians 5:22 KJV)

Good deeds come from a good heart. Goodness is the best of all human qualities in action: thoughtfulness, truthfulness, sympathy, fairness, kindness, unselfishness, helpfulness, generosity, tolerance, and forgiveness. Goodness is yard work for the neighbor whose back is hurting. It is cleaning for the woman who has recently had surgery. Goodness is medicine for the sick and food for the hungry. It is forgiveness for the offender. It is a helping hand for the fallen. Goodness is encouragement for the discouraged and a song to the hopeless.

Matthew 7:12 shows the Golden Rule in practice: doing unto others as you would have them do unto you. Goodness makes the world a better place. Goodness sees others and appreciates them. Goodness hears the cries of the needy and the brokenhearted. Goodness bears one another's burdens. Goodness helps the struggling. By being good to others, we are good to ourselves. When we have God living inside our hearts, we have the power within to do good.

> Oh, taste and see that the Lord is good; blessed is the man who trusts in Him. (Psalm 34:8 NKJV)

Our existence and goodness depends on God—our Creator and Redeemer.

Women show their love for God by doing good works rather than an outward show of elaborate hairstyles, gold, pearls or expensive apparel (1 Timothy 2:9–10). A woman is a representative of God; therefore, she should always try to look her best. Nonetheless, her looks should not affirm her love for God. The heart of God's daughters should "be as cornerstones, polished after the similitude of a palace" (Psalm 144:12 KJV). Her heart should offer the best, with gratitude for all things. She should be full of kindness and tenderhearted. A woman of God should be known by her good works—not her looks.

> Beauty is vain; but a woman that fears the Lord
> she shall be praised. (Proverbs 31:30 KJV)

Mankind looks at the outward appearance, but God sees the heart. 1 Samuel 25:3 speaks of Abigail as being a good-looking woman, but she did not try to pacify David with her beauty. Her intention was not to flaunt her good looks. David had murder on his mind, and no matter how good-looking Abigail may have appeared at the time, her looks were not going to appease him. Abigail went out to meet David and capture his heart through her kind words and actions. Abigail understood that doing what is right is what God required of her.

I observed someone's reaction to a man who was asking for a handout on a street corner. The man was yelled at and treated as though some deadly plague was on him—and he was not given anything. In the end, it was not the beggar's appearance that looked ugly. The ugliness was seen in the person who could have shown kindness but chose not to. Ugliness depicts the opposite of kindness.

A woman of wise understanding comprehends the meaning of kindness and is generous in her giving.

> One gives freely, yet grows all the richer, another
> withholds that what she should give, and only
> suffers want. (Proverbs 11:24 ESV)

Abigail made haste in preparing the best of her substance, and she gave in abundance. In humbleness, Abigail gave generously unto David and his men.

In order to be a giver, one must first have a willing heart.

Teach me to do Your will; for You are my God:
Your Spirit is good; lead me into the land of
uprightness. (Psalm 143:10 NKJV)

Abigail gave out of a willing heart. She understood that giving
to those in need is giving unto the Lord. By giving, she would be
blessed. She understood that God does not ask us to give so that
others are eased and we are burdened. It is only fair to share when
we have so much and others have so little. We serve a just God.

Those who gathered too much had nothing left.
Those who gathered only a little had all they
needed. (2 Corinthians 8:15 CEV)

When our hearts and souls are set to seek the Lord, we will give
as God directs. We will not give grudgingly or of necessity. God
loves a cheerful giver. God looks at the heart and sees the intent
of the giver. I am reminded of the words of an old hymn, "You
can't beat God giving—no matter how hard you try." God set the
ultimate example of giving.

For God so loved the world that He gave His only
begotten Son, that whosoever believes in Him
shall not perish, but have everlasting life. (John
3:16 KJV)

To focus on doing that which is right, a woman must first think
right.

For as he thinks in his heart, so is he. (Proverbs
23:7 NKJV)

If we want to have wise understanding, we must center our
thoughts on "things that are true, honest, just, lovely, pure, lovely

and of a good report; if there be any goodness, and if there be any praise, think on these things" (Philippians 4:8 KJV). One cannot watch whatever comes across the movie screen, listen to whatever comes on the radio, or read whatever novel sounds good. Whatever you focus your thoughts on is what you become. If you want to be more loving, don't watch movies that are filled with hatred. If you want to be a grateful person, don't listen to songs filled with all the wants of the world. If you want to be more like Christ, don't read scandal magazines. Instead, read your Bible.

> Bring into captivity every thought to the obedience
> of Christ. (2 Corinthians 10:5 KJV)

When our minds begin to wander in the wrong direction, we must think of Jesus. His thoughts are higher than our thoughts, and His ways are not our ways. When we begin to focus our thoughts on Jesus, our characters will become more like His—and we will be honest in our dealings with others.

> Love our enemies, we will bless those who curse
> us, we will do good to those who hate us and
> we will pray for those who spitefully use us and
> persecute us. (Matthew 5:44 KJV)

Abigail's thoughts about her husband were probably not always good thoughts. I'm sure that living with Nabal was not easy. At those times, we have to learn to bring every thought captive and think about good and pleasant things—things that are lovely and of a good report. There are times when we must leave our bitter thoughts at the feet of Jesus and allow the mind that is in Christ Jesus to be in us (Philippians 2:5).

Abigail was honest with David. Although she was very wealthy, she didn't come before him as though she were rich and famous. Abigail came before David in humbleness, bowing before him at his feet. She didn't try to cover up her husband's actions and make excuses for his behavior. In humility, she told David that her husband had acted foolishly, and she asked David to put Nabal's foolish actions upon her. There was no pride in her attitude. It was a display of a pure heart.

David noticed that Abigail was a woman with an upright heart. He also regarded her as a woman who came with a good report of Godly peace. God will keep you in perfect peace—whose mind is stayed on Him (Isaiah 26:3). When your thoughts are centered on Christ, the peace of God, which surpasses all understanding, will keep your mind on things that are true, honest, just, pure, lovely, and of good report. This was the mind that Abigail portrayed.

Abigail's words and actions demonstrated her thoughts, which were exemplified through power and excellence.

> Who can find a virtuous woman? For her price is
> far above rubies. (Proverbs 31:10 KJV)

Abigail came before David with a bold and excellent spirit. A virtuous woman is one who understands the power behind her actions. She understands that her goodness comes from God who holds the universe in place.

CHAPTER 3

Understanding Knowledge

To goodness, add knowledge. Fear of the Lord conveys a positive holy reverence, an attitude of respect.

> The fear of the Lord is the beginning of knowledge.
> (Proverbs 1:7 KJV)

A healthy fear of God includes the fear of the consequences of disobedience. We insult the spirit of grace and fall into the hands of the living God who said, "Vengeance is mine. I will repay."

God is great, and to Him alone we give honor, majesty, and glory; for righteous are all His ways! God is everything and in everything.

> Where can I go from Your Spirit? Or where can I flee from Your presence? If I ascend into heaven, You are there; if I make my bed in hell, behold, You are there. If I take the wings of the morning, and dwell in the uttermost parts of the sea, even there Your hand shall lead me, and Your right hand shall hold me. (Psalm 139:7–10 NKJV)

For my thoughts are not your thoughts, neither are your ways my ways, says the Lord. For as the heavens are higher than your ways, and my thoughts than your thoughts. (Isaiah 55:8–9 KJV)

Such knowledge is too wonderful for me; it is high, I cannot attain it. (Psalm 139:6 KJV)

We stand in awe when we reverence the Lord in the beauty of His holiness—to which is the beginning of knowledge.

But we have the mind of Christ. (1 Corinthians 2:16 KJV)

God reveals Himself to us through His Holy Spirit.

I have told you everything my Father has told me. (John 15:15 CEV)

Jesus reveals Himself to us through His Word. Knowledge of scripture is knowledge of Christ. Before we read the Bible, we must ask God to open our hearts to His Word. By praying and meditating, God begins to renew our minds—and the mind of Christ begins to be in us.

Colossians 3:10 (KJV) says that we are "renewed in knowledge." Philippians 2:5 (KJV) says that we are to "let this mind be in you, which was also in Christ Jesus."

The more we study God's Word, the more we become like Christ. Renewal of the mind does not happen overnight. It is a growing process.

Study to show thyself approved unto God, a workman that needeth not to be ashamed, rightly dividing the word of truth. (2 Timothy 2:15 KJV)

More Word, more God—yet knowledge puffs up. People do not care how much we know until they know how much we care. Therefore, we are to "be doers of the Word and not hearers only" (James 1:22 KJV). If we only take in the Word and never act upon it, James 1:23–24 says that we become as someone who observes themselves in a mirror; walks away, and then forgets what he or she looks like. We are to be the reflection of Christ for the world to see. Therefore, if we forget who we reflect, how will the world know Christ through us?

> You do err, not knowing the scriptures, nor the power of God. (Matthew 22:29 KJV)

God wants us to read His Word, and He wants us to study His Word and hide it in our hearts so that we might not sin against Him (Psalm 119:11). We are to meditate on the scriptures and memorize them. By doing so, we are allowing the mind that is in Christ Jesus to also be in us. The heart that hides God's Word is to be guarded with all diligence, for out of it flow the issues of life (Proverbs 4:23).

> Oh, that they had such a heart in them that they would fear Me and always keep all My commandments, that it might be well with them and with their children forever. (Deuteronomy 5:29 NKJV)

God's Word will be health for our whole body (Proverbs 4:23). We are also to tell our children of His commandments. We are to teach them diligently and talk of them when we sit in the house, when we are out walking, when we lie down, and when we rise. We are to write them on our hands, on our foreheads, on our doorposts, and on our gates so that our children may keep His commandments and learn to fear the Lord our God (Deuteronomy 6:7–9).

In this country, it is a privilege that Bibles are readily available. In other parts of the world, Bibles are scarce. What about people who have come to know Christ as their personal Lord and Savior but do not own Bibles to learn what God commands of us? Jesus spoke about this matter to Thomas.

> Because you have seen me, you have believed: blessed are they that have not seen, and yet have believed. (John 20:29 KJV)

Jesus was saying that believing gives you life through His name. Jesus is the Word. Before Moses was inspired by God to begin writing Genesis, the Word existed. In fact, the Word existed before God created the universe.

> In the beginning was the Word, and the Word was with God, and the Word was God. (John 1:1 KJV)

God is the Word, yet God goes beyond that understanding and calls Himself "I Am That I Am" (Exodus 3:14 KJV). If you want to know the Word, get to know the Great I Am. Abigail knew the Great I Am.

Through Abigail's knowledge of God, she was able to share in God's divine nature as He shined His grace and peace upon her. God's grace stopped David from killing her family, and God's peace turned David's heart. It takes a woman of wise understanding to recognize that knowledge is a divine gift that is pleasant to the soul. Through the knowledge of God, we are given all things that pertain to life and godliness by God's divine power (2 Peter 1:3).

> God is not a man that He should lie. (Numbers 23:19 KJV)

Therefore, since God gives us all things pertaining to life and godliness, if we have not, it is because we ask not. And if we ask and do not receive, it is because we ask amiss; we ask with the wrong intentions (James 4:2–3). If we want knowledge, we are to "ask God who gives generously to all without reproach; and it will be given to him" (James 1:5 ESV). If we seek understanding as searching for silver, and as for hidden treasures, then we shall understand the fear of the Lord, and find the knowledge of God.

> For the Lord gives wisdom and out of His mouth comes knowledge and understanding. (Proverbs 2:4–6 KJV)

Abigail sought knowledge because she knew the value of knowledge was greater than silver. In Abigail's search for knowledge, she obtained it; along with knowledge came favor, peace, and understanding. Abigail sought knowledge through her reverence for the Lord. In 1 Samuel 25:26, Abigail reverenced God, and God revealed to her that it was He who stopped David from killing her family. She did not credit this act of grace and mercy to herself. She credited the Lord. It was only through God's mercy and grace that Abigail was warned of Nabal's harsh words toward David. It was through God's mercy, grace, and sovereignty that Abigail prepared to meet David with the necessary provisions.

David wrote in Psalm 23 that God's goodness and mercy follow him all the days of his life. When we feel as though the enemy is trying to push us back trying to make us fall, always remember that we are about to bump into God's goodness and mercy that follow us. We serve a mighty God who will never leave us or forsake us. We reverence God by giving Him all the credit, realizing that God is worthy of all praise. It is not our doing. It is to God for whom all glory is due.

I am the Lord: that is my name: and my glory I
will not give to another. (Isaiah 43:8 KJV)

How could Abigail be so humble at a time like that? She knew who
she was fighting. Ephesians 6:10–18 tells us that our fight is not
against humans. We are fighting against forces and authorities.
We are fighting against rulers of darkness and powers in the
spiritual world. Abigail understood that she was not fighting
against Nabal or David. She was fighting against spiritual forces,
and she knew she had to be strong in the Lord and the power of
His might. Knowledge provides the power to overcome the enemy
and understand who the enemy is. When we understand who the
enemy is—and realize that he is out to kill, steal, and destroy—we
arm ourselves for the invisible battle that dangerously rages all
around us. We recognize that the strategies the enemy uses against
us, are to bring turmoil to everything that matters most to us: our
minds, our emotions, our families, and our futures.

Ephesians 6:10–18 also tells us that when we fight, we are to
put on the full armor of God so that we will be able to resist in
the evil day; and having done everything, we are to stand firm.
We prepare for an attack by standing firm in God's truth. When
the enemy attacks us with lies to get us to doubt God's Word, we
stand strong and choose to believe and trust God and act on what
His Word says.

When we put on the breastplate of righteousness, we do
what is right in our hearts, thereby guarding our hearts so that
we will not sin against God. When we stand firm with our feet
anchored, we are prepared with the gospel of peace. When the
enemy comes against us, we will be able to stand and not slip.
We have a supernatural ability to resist fear, remain calm, and
stand confidently on God's Word until we receive a breakthrough.
While standing firm, we take up the shield of faith that protects
us from head to toe, guarding us from the burning arrows and the
lies the enemy tells us. While standing firm, we put on the helmet

of salvation that guards our minds and our thoughts. We will not be conformed to this world because what we think will determine what we believe, what we believe will determine what we do, and what we do will determine how we live. As we continue to stand firm, we take up the sword of the Spirit, which is the Word of God.

> For the Word of God is living, and powerful, and sharper than any two-edged sword, piercing even to the division of soul and spirit, and of the joints and marrow, and is a discerner of the thoughts and intents of the heart. (Hebrews 4:12 NKJV)

The Word is powerful and effective in every situation we face because God's Word contains the power to deliver us. Hebrews 6:18 says that we are to pray at all times with all prayers and petitions in the Spirit according to God's Word, which produces results, bringing forth dramatic, life-giving changes to areas where breakthroughs are needed. Let us not be overtaken by the schemes of the enemy. Let us understand that we are to stand strong and equipped in the power of God. Abigail came before David—armed and dangerous for battle against principalities, the powers of darkness, and the rulers of this world.

Proverbs 1:22 (KJV) says that "fools hate knowledge." Nabal was not seeking knowledge, which is why his mouth fed on foolishness and he spoke curses into existence. I once heard it said that before we give anyone a piece of our mind, we ought to make sure that we can get by with what we might have left. Nabal did not understand that he was doomed for his lack of knowledge; if he had understood, he would have known that his prideful talk would lead to destruction and his haughty spirit would proceed his fall (Proverbs 16:18). God resists the proud. To the haughty, He does not share His grace.

Abigail responded to knowledge with wisdom. Knowledge is the rare trait of learning with perception, discovering, and growing. Wisdom is the ability to understand knowledge, see with discernment, and view life as God perceives it.

> Wisdom is the principle thing; therefore get wisdom: and with all thy getting get understanding. (Proverbs 4:7 KJV)

Understanding is the ability to respond to knowledge with wisdom. It took wisdom for Abigail to follow the best course of action, based on her knowledge and understanding.

When Abigail acquired knowledge of Nabal and David's situation, she perceived that David needed to be appeased in order for peace to abound.

> If it is possible, as much as depends on you, live peaceably with all men. (Romans 12:18 NKJV)

To establish a growing atmosphere of peace, she needed God's wisdom to guide her.

> For God is not the author of confusion, but of peace. (1 Corinthians 14:33 KJV)

Abigail knew that if there was going to be any peace in the resolution of the situation, the peace had to come by doing things God's way—and not allowing herself to get in the way. It is a privilege for a woman to know and believe that God will do what is just and fair. God is holy, righteous, and full of grace and mercy.

CHAPTER 4

Understanding Self-Control

To knowledge, add self-control. Self-control is the ability to hold your peace in the midst of adversity. David exemplified self-control when he was given opportunities to kill Saul, but he spared Saul's life because Saul was the king. Jesus demonstrated self-control when He stood before Pilate and answered not a word—and even Pilate marveled.

Abigail exemplified self-control when she told Nabal not a word but went about doing that which was right for the sake of peace. Her actions toward David validated a clear head and calm disposition. Her kind words proved her to be thoughtful.

> She opens her mouth with wisdom; and on her tongue is the law of kindness. (Psalm 31:26 NKJV)

Abigail pondered her words spoken to David. Her desire was to bring about peace and not offend David.

> A word fitly spoken is like apples of gold in pictures of silver. (Proverbs 25:11 KJV)

In our dealings with irrational people, we may be called to carry the blame in order to have peace in our lives so that God may be glorified.

Abigail was the opposite of her husband. He lacked any kind of self-control. Nabal could not control his drinking, his behavior, or his mouth, which he used as a deadly poison to evoke strife and contention.

Peace resists strife and contention, and it does not demand its own will. To avoid strife and contention, one must submit to God. We argue because we want to be right. People must give up their rights so that God may be right. Submission unto God is a process that is to be learned daily. In 1 Corinthians 15:31 (KJV), Paul said, "I die daily." Submission unto God is dying to self daily.

> For what I am doing, I do not understand. For what I will to do, that I do not practice; but what I hate, that I do. (Romans 7:15 NKJV)

When we die to self, God is glorified—and sin does not dominate us. In dying to self, we can say, "It is not my will. God, let Your will be done in my life." Strife and contention are not the nature of a woman who personifies self-control. Rather, she strives for harmony, goodwill, and ways that will bring about peace in relationships.

In order to have peace, there are times when a woman has to keep silent.

> Be still and know that I am God. (Psalm 46:10 KJV)

In order to hear from God, we must be quiet.

> He leads me beside the still waters. (Psalm 23:2b NKJV)

When I reflect upon still waters, I think of quietness, peace, and serenity. We must keep in mind that serenity is not always peace from the storm. It is peace amidst the storm. When all hell seems to be breaking loose, God will give you peace.

> Thou will keep him in perfect peace, whose mind
> is stayed on Thee. (Isaiah 26:3 KJV)

Where peace is lacking, you can be assured that the enemy is involved. Peace is twofold: internal peace within oneself and external peace that one upholds with others. If you have internal peace with God and self, it will produce an outward peace with men. The one who avoids strife and contention learns self-control.

Once again, God spoke to me in a dream. Throughout the night, He continually woke me up with the word *contention*. At the time, I didn't know what the word even meant. I had always heard the word mentioned along with the word *strife*. I knew that strife meant arguing, but what did contention mean? I went to *Webster's Dictionary* and read that contention is what causes strife. At the time, I had a legitimate reason for bringing up a rightful discussion that always seemed to end up in strife with my husband. God was saying, "Only by pride cometh contention" (Proverbs 13:10 KJV). I knew that the discussion that I was continually bringing up to my husband was going to end in strife. Therefore, I needed to let go and give the issue to God.

> God is not the author of confusion. (1 Corinthians
> 14:33 KJV)

I had to learn to leave my contentious issues at God's feet. Before I could lay the issue of my husband at God's feet, I had to lay myself there. I had to learn to trust God with my emotions and my inward and sometimes private issues so that I would not be robbed of my joy.

> The joy of the Lord is your strength. (Nehemiah
> 8:10 KJV)

God created us, and He knows how to manage us if we allow Him to do so. God wants us to talk to Him about everything; there is nothing too hard for God to handle.

God can handle what we cannot. I once worked with a woman who went home, got in the bathtub with a blanket, and blew her brains out. We must not try to carry our burdens alone. God will bear our burdens, if we give them to Him. We must learn to let go and let God, which is God's will.

As I was driving, I saw a woman walking her dog and waiting for an opportune time to cross the street. The dog was anxious to cross the street, and the lady was trying to hold the dog back. She walked out in front of an oncoming car. The car used the bike lane to pass behind her to avoid hitting her. The woman showed no emotion. She evidently had lost self-control of her emotions, which caused her to lose her will to live.

Abigail's heart was to do the will of God. She called God her Lord. When God is our Lord, we allow Him to lead us. When we are our own lord, we will do things our way—the way we want it. When we allow God to be the Lord of our lives, God will make our enemies be at peace with us (Proverbs 16:7). When we allow God to be our Lord, we will no longer be in control of ourselves.

Self-control is a means of overcoming evil inclinations and using moderation in life daily. Self-control resists gluttony, lust, drunkenness, gossip, outbursts of temper; even good things when taken in excess: work, play, and thrift.

> Wherefore, my beloved brethren, let every man be
> swift to hear, slow to speak, slow to wrath. (James
> 1:19 KJV)

> But whosoever shall smite thee on thy right cheek,
> turn to him the other also. (Matthew 5:39 KJV)

> And be not drunk with wine, wherein is excess;
> but be filled with the Spirit. (Ephesians 4:18 KJV)

> This I say then, walk in the Spirit and you shall not
> fulfill the lust of the flesh. (Galatians 5:16 KJV)

> He that ruleth his spirit [is greater] than he that
> taketh a city. (Proverbs 16:32 KJV)

Unless you rule yourself, you will be ruled by others and circumstances. Wilma Rudolph contracted polio at the age of four and was told by her doctor that she would never walk again. Her mother told her that she would walk, and Wilma believed her mother. With much physical therapy, she began to walk. By the time she entered high school, she was running. She received a college scholarship for track and field, went to the Olympics, and won three gold medals. She was acclaimed for being the fastest woman in the world in the 1960s. That is self-control.

> And every man that strives for the mastery is
> temperate in all things. Now they do it to obtain
> a corruptible crown; but we, an incorruptible. (1
> Corinthians 9:25 KJV)

An incorruptible crown is the crown of life, which is obtained through the precious blood of Christ Jesus. For this He suffered the shame of the cross so that by this we may inherit eternal life. For on that day, to all who have finished the race and kept the faith, there is laid up a crown of righteousness, which the Lord, the righteous Judge, will give to all that love His appearing.

It is God who gives the righteous self-control. He causes them to be as bold as lions and as meek as lambs. Abigail rode out to meet David boldly, and she approached him as meekly as a lamb. In her heart, Abigail was determined to do the right thing. When doing God's will, we have to make up our minds to serve God. We cannot be wishy-washy. An unstable person receives nothing from God.

> A double-minded man is unstable in all his ways.
> (James 1:8 KJV)

He is like a wave in the sea, tossed to and fro. God wants us to have a yes-or-no mentality.

> Let our yes be yes, and our no be no. (James 5:12 NKJV)

With Abigail, it wasn't a question of whether she should go or not. Abigail wanted to do God's perfect will, when she went. She had a heart to do what was right, and God gave her the courage to do it.

Courage is being confident that God will be your shield—no matter what happens. Abigail placed her confidence in God and not in herself. When she rode out to meet David, she was not going to join him for tea. She was going to face an angry man who had revenge and murder on his mind. Doing that took guts! In times like these, we need God to be in control.

> Not by power, nor by might, but by my Spirit, says the Lord of host. (Zechariah 4:6 KJV)

CHAPTER 5

Understanding Patience

To self-control, add patience. Patience is the ability to endure long without complaining, and is produced by facing adversity. Abigail personified patience as she faced adversity caused by Nabal's rude and obnoxious behavior.

> Boast of our troubles, because we know that trouble produces endurance, endurance brings God's approval, and His approval creates hope. This hope does not disappoint us, for God has poured out His love into our hearts by means of His Holy Spirit, who is God's gift to us. (Romans 5:3–5 GNT)

This hope is demonstrated through stories I have heard concerning the Holocaust and the Rwandan genocide. Survivors tell stories of brutality, torture, and murder. These survivors emerged with stories of how God transformed their hearts to love and forgive their perpetrators. They shared heart-wrenching stories of God's enduring love as their spirits were purged of hatred amid the evil of this world. Their stories tell how God's strength sustained them as Christ's Spirit and words became their guide through times of profound horror. Although they could not change their situations, they allowed God to change them. These stories tell of the glory of God and how God will bring you through with faith and patience.

> Rejoicing in hope, patient in tribulation. (Romans 12:12 KJV)

Through troublesome times, we become stronger. We come to rely on God's strength instead of our own strength. Some might say that this is how and when we develop thick skin. At that time, we come to realize that what used to bother us no longer bothers us.

Through patience, we will learn to accept blessings in any form. I heard a story about a young man who had just graduated from high school and was excited to receive his graduation present: a new car that had been promised to him by his father. After the graduation ceremony, the father took the son aside and told him that he wanted to give him his present. To the son's surprise, his father handed him a Bible instead of a car. The father told the son that he hoped he would read the Bible often and that he would use it as his guide. The son could not contain his anger. He went to his room, threw down the Bible, gathered a few belongings, and set off to discover his own way. For years, he did not return home. He kept in contact with his mother. When the son was notified of his father's death, he finally returned home. His old bedroom was still kept the way he had left it. He came upon the Bible that his father had given him for graduation. Thumbing through it, he came across an envelope with his name on it. He opened it and found a check for the amount of the car he had been hoping for. Along with the check, there was a note from his father: "I thought that you would like to pick out your own car." When we are unable to change life circumstances or take back hurtful words, we end up with regret.

I have learned that in whatsoever state I am in,
to be content. (Philippians 4:11 KJV)

By following Paul's example of contentment, we will be able to look at the past without regret, the present without envy, and the future without fear. If we look with regret, we become depressed. If we look with envy, we become jealous. If we look with fear, we become stuck. Contentment brings forth patience, and impatience brings forth regret.

> My brothers and sisters count it all joy when you fall into various trials, knowing that the testing of your faith produces patience. But let patience have her perfect work, that you may be perfect and complete, lacking nothing. (James 1:2–4 NKJV)

Abigail did not run from adversity; she faced it. She faced her trials through the strength of God; she became a woman of wisdom who possessed wise intelligence, and she exhibited strength through her trials. When we find ourselves stuck between a rock and a hard place, we must not rely on our own strength; we must rely on the strength of God. Through various trials, the lessons from the school of hard knocks will help us to move forward on our journeys.

In life, we find that there is a lesson with every trial. If the lesson is not learned, we go through a period of *recycling*: a way to recover by passing through a cycle again for checking or treating. Trials are repeated because we did not learn our lessons the first time. Without patience, we rush through trials to avoid pain as much as possible. We find ourselves in similar situations because we did not learn our lessons during the first trials. When we go through trials, we must question the Lord about what we are to learn. God does not do things through happenstance. God is a God of purpose who allows things for our good. Trials come to make us strong and to find our strength in God. It is through our problems that we learn to call on God and depend on Him to solve them.

Have you ever observed someone lacking patience? They don't take the time to think. They just react. When people lack patience, they think more of themselves than of others. Jesus did the opposite. He exemplified patience by being meek and humble. The disciples wanted to remove the children from Jesus's presence, but He told His disciples to suffer the little children to come unto Him, for such is the kingdom of heaven (Matthew 19:14). Jesus was telling His disciples to be patient with the children and become like them.

In another parable, the disciples were hungry. The Pharisees rebuked them for plucking corn on the Sabbath, which was against the law. Jesus told the Pharisees that mercy is better than sacrifice. Jesus demonstrated patience through compassion. He taught that mercy is above following the law. When we allow patience to work, we become perfect and complete. We become reflections of Christ.

Nabal lacked patience and was rude, bad-tempered, and evil in all of his doings. When Abigail approached David, she spoke the truth concerning her husband by humbly stating what was on her heart:

> Please sir, let me take the blame. Please, don't pay any attention to Nabal, that good-for-nothing! He is exactly what his name means—a fool!" (1 Samuel 25:24–25 GNT)

Abigail carried the blame, and she spoke the truth concerning her husband. It was not in a disrespectful way, and she understood that the truth would make her free.

> Everyone must be quick to listen, but slow to speak and slow to become angry. (James 1:19 GNT)

As Abigail rode out to meet David, she must have pondered in her heart just exactly what she would say to him. In upsetting times, our minds are filled with words that express our heartfelt feelings. But rather than saying what we feel, we need to pray and ask God to give us the words to say.

Patience in speech honors God. Therefore, we must pray and allow God to direct our speech. For as men and women think in their hearts, so are they; what is in the heart will come out.

While waiting on the Lord, we must possess a servant attitude that is bent toward pleasing God. How does one serve the Lord pleasingly while waiting? Whatever we do for the Lord must come from our hearts. First of all, to serve while waiting does not mean sitting idly. If a waiter served me in a lazy manner with a bad attitude, my assumption would be that the waiter needed an attitude adjustment. While we wait on the Lord, let us serve with a spirit of excellence and a cheerful heart so that others may see our good works and glorify God (Matthew 5:16).

We must learn to patiently wait on God while He makes a way in His timing. What if God's timing turns into years? Do we still wait—or do we take matters into our own hands? During extended waiting times, God says, "Be still and know that I am God" (Psalm 46:10 KJV).

We learn to be still and wait on the Lord when we come to the realization that God does not operate in our time frame. He does not move when we want Him too. We live in a microwave generation that wants it now!

> One day with the Lord is as a thousand years, and
> a thousand years as one day. (2 Peter 3:8 KJV)

We must be very careful about rushing God's timing. We never know who or what He is protecting or saving us from.

I was having the oil changed before heading to an appointment in another town. The person servicing my car went to the store to purchase an item for the oil change. The place was a well-established business, and I thought this was rather odd. Instead of becoming impatient and focusing on the fact that I might be late for my appointment, I decided to possess a patient attitude. After the oil change, I headed to my destination and came across a terrible car accident. As I was slowly driving by the scene of the crash, I prayed for those involved in the collision and thanked God that it was not me. Through patience, God's grace and mercy spared me from an accident that I could have been involved in.

As we wait patiently with our hearts bent for God, we are given opportunities to notice things that otherwise might have gone unnoticed.

> He makes me to lie down in green pastures:
> he leads me beside the still waters. (Psalm 23:2
> NKJV)

It's reminiscent of sitting on a park bench and observing. We have an opportunity to see trees, beautiful flowers, a beautiful sky; and let us not miss the rainbow. We see people with friendly faces greeting one another, and we know in our hearts that they are showing love to one another.

Life is filled with so much to be thankful for. Without patience, we can become so caught up in the cares of this world that we become dulled to God's goodness toward us. When we are patient, we are allowed to know and appreciate God. We become grateful through our appreciation.

> In everything give thanks: for this is the will of God
> in Christ Jesus concerning you. (1 Thessalonians
> 5:18 KJV)

God wants us to be thankful for all things—the good and the bad. No matter how bad our situations may appear, they could always be worse. A man complained about having to walk to work and then he saw a man with no legs. The thing that appears unpleasant to us might be someone else's blessing. Another man said that, after tying his shoes in the morning, everything after that was a piece of cake. He only had one arm. By being patiently grateful, we are able to experience the peace of God, which surpasses all knowledge.

When Abigail patiently approached David, her quiet spirit sparked David's attention. A gentle and quiet spirit is precious in the sight of God. It represents meekness—strength that is under control. Through patience, we acquire controlled strength.

> Be anxious for nothing, but in everything by prayer and supplication, with thanksgiving, let your request be made known to God; and the peace of God, which surpasses all understanding, will guard your hearts and minds through Christ Jesus. (Philippians 4:6 NKJV)

Anxiety is the absence of patience and lays the groundwork for stress. I chuckled to myself when I heard someone describe stress as "the confusion created when one's mind overrides the body's desire to choke the living daylights out of some jerk who desperately needs it." Stress is simply a reaction to a stimulus that disturbs our physical or mental equilibrium. When everything seems to have become too much, our minds are overloaded. We must think about the Lord and react in a righteous manner.

The way we react to things affects us emotionally and physically. After Abigail settled matters with David, she told Nabal what had almost transpired. After hearing the news, Nabal's heart literally failed him. Nabal's reaction to hearing what David had planned to do to him was an example of a physical response to stress.

To have patience in our lives, we should pray: Lord, help me to change the things that I can, help me to accept the things that I cannot change, and give me the wisdom to know the difference. If Abigail had tried to do things her way—rather than God's way—she would have missed God's peace and the opportunity to become David's wife. A woman of good understanding places her trust in God, believing that He will work all things out for her good.

Patience is having the ability to keep a good attitude while waiting. Proverbs 14:29 says that love is patient. Therefore, patience reflects a loving attitude. Patience is demonstrated while waiting for someone with a cane to cross the street. Patience is offering a parking space to another car after you have waited for it. Patience is choosing not to be annoyed by the physical handicaps that slow others down. A patient spirit does not demonstrate road rage. A patient spirit shows courtesy. Patience is thinking more highly of others than self. Patience is showing love in action.

We pay a price when we lack patience. Rather than taking the time to pray, we jump ahead of God and do things our way, which inevitably turns out to be the wrong way. We end up taking the wrong turn in life—only to end up at the destination of regret. Without patience, we find ourselves pondering the what-ifs of life. If only I had waited! Impatience draws us away from God. Patience reveals a heart that trusts and is confident in the Lord. Patience can be hard, but God shows Himself strong in our weakness. Through patience, we become more like Christ.

Patience is a fruit of the Spirit that exemplifies Christ in us— our hope of glory. When we exemplify a patient spirit, the world sees Christ in us.

> Trust in the Him with all your heart, and lean not on your own understanding; in all your ways acknowledge Him, and He shall direct your paths. (Proverbs 3:5–6 NKJV)

Have you ever tried to use your strength to lift a heavy object all by yourself? We strain and we grunt. Not until we rely on God's strength, do we truly understand the Scripture:

> Not by might, nor by power, but my Spirit, says the
> Lord of Host. (Zechariah 4:6 NKJV)

God does not want us groaning in our own strength. He wants us to patiently trust in Him for all things because all things are His.

If we were to patiently realize that all things are God's, we would be able to view our needs and wants similar to a grocery store in heaven. On the shelves, we would find faith, salvation, God's Holy Spirit, strength, courage, grace, love, understanding, wisdom, prayer, peace, joy, songs, and praises. Philippians 4:19 tells us that God will supply all our needs according to His riches in glory by Christ Jesus. When God says all things, He is not simply talking about monetary things. Through patience, we receive everything from God freely because Jesus has already paid for it all.

Sometimes we don't even know what we need. We find ourselves saying, "Lord, help me." Benjamin Franklin said, "God helps those who help themselves." That quote is incorrect. God helps those who admit that they are helpless. If we try to do it all by ourselves, God will step back and say, "Go right ahead."

God will not force His help on us. We need God. God does not need us. Through patience, we come to realize this.

CHAPTER 6

Understanding Devotion to God

To patience, add devotion to God. A woman who understands devotion to God sets herself apart for His purpose. The definition of devotion is "love, loyalty, or enthusiasm for an eagerness to stand up for the cause."

Years ago, my thoughts began to always be on God. At the time, I felt as though I was different. I thought I was the only one feeling that way. One day, a friend of mine stated that Jesus was always on her mind—as He must also be for others. I came to realize that the love relationship I shared with Christ was experienced by others as well. It was a joyous feeling to realize that others loved God and always had Him on their minds—just as I did.

On my lunch hour, Jesus and I would go for walks. During these walks, I started to experience nature in a new way. The sun shone brighter, the trees appeared greener, and the birds sang louder. I began to see God in all my surroundings. In my conversations with others, God was there. As I greeted people on the street, God was there. He was always on my mind, in everything I did, and everywhere I went He was there. I felt that I had a secret joy that others did not know of. There was a joy inside of me that was bubbling over.

The more I read my Bible, the greater my desire grew to know God. The hours spent with God were never long enough. Years later, that feeling is even stronger. I jokingly tell others that God loves me so much, but He loves them too. When we have a love relationship with God, He will make us feel as though we are the apples of His eye—and we are.

> Draw near to God and He will draw near to you.
> (James 4:8 NKJV)

I drew near to God, and God's Holy Spirit became my intimate and beloved companion. Through our relationship, I came to understand that God's Holy Spirit is a person and not a force or an influence.

> When He, the Spirit of truth, is come, He will
> guide you into all truth. (John 16:13 KJV)

The Holy Spirit is a person who thinks, feels, communicates, perceives, and responds. He gives and receives love. He is gentle and loving.

> Love the Lord your God with all our heart, with
> all your soul, with all your mind, and with all your
> strength: This is the first commandment. (Mark
> 12:30 NKJV)

Jesus loved us so much that He died for us; through His death, we became free from sin. Freedom is not free; what will our love for God cost?

Rachel Joy Scott was martyr at Columbine High School. After her death, Rachel's family discovered her personal journals. They revealed a deep, secret relationship with Jesus that even her family knew little about. Rachel's walk with Jesus displayed wisdom far beyond her years, and she actually seemed to foreshadow her death in several entries. Here is an excerpt from her personal journal written on April 20, 1998.

> I am not going to apologize for speaking the name of Jesus,
> I am not going to justify my faith to them,
> And I am not going to hide the light that God has put into me.
> If I have to sacrifice everything ... I will. I will take it.

Rachael's bloodstained journal was delayed in being returned to her family for weeks after her death because it was in her backpack when she died. One of the bullets that passed through her small body was discovered inside her backpack and was considered police evidence until it was officially released. Rachel's journal clearly reveals that she was fervent in her desire to serve God, and her love for God cost her life.

Are we really fervent for God—or is it just lip service? How much of God do we really desire? Do we want the Lord to come into our lives? Do we desire a one-way relationship where God is only allowed to speak when asked? Do we go about doing our own thing, not allowing God to interrupt unless our backs are up against a wall and we can't seem to find a way out on our own? Do we find ourselves calling on God as a last result? Do we meet God at church on Sunday, spend one or two hours with Him, and leave Him there until next Sunday? Do we go to church on Sunday seeking a good feeling but not a changed heart? Do we distance ourselves from God because we aren't sure what He may ask of us?

Paul's desire was to know the Lord and he was shipwrecked, beaten, and left for dead.

And this, so that I may know Him … and [that
I may share] the fellowship of His sufferings, by
being continually conformed [inwardly into His
likeness even] to His death [dying as He did]; so
that I may attain to the resurrection [that will
raise me] from the dead. (Philippians 3:10)

He counted his losses as dung that he may win
Christ. (Philippians 3:8 KJV)

Are we willing to partake of Christ's suffering so that we may
know Him? Being willing to pay the price, Abigail took on Nabal's
sin and was viewed as a woman who wanted to please God.

To participate in Christ's suffering, we must have hearts bent
to pleasing and not sinning against God. A scenario that always
comes to my mind when I think of sinning against God is white-
water rafting. At first, the water moves smoothly as you gently use
your oars to row the boat down the river and take in the beautiful
scenery. The sun is shining, the sky is blue, and there is not a
cloud in sight. A gentle breeze keeps the warm rays of sunshine
from forming beads of perspiration upon your forehead. *What a
beautiful world!* You become confident in your rafting skills. *I've
got this!* As the current slowly moves the boat toward shore, you
start to feel as though you no longer need the oars. You throw your
oars into the water, thinking they will just drift back to shore—
and you'll be okay without them. That is when the white water
becomes treacherous. You've seen it in the movies. Just around
the bend, the water begins to rush toward a frightening noise. You
discover that the noise is connected to a cascading waterfall. You
are about to topple over it without any oars to steer away from it.
This is an example of how sin creeps in. You become oblivious to
the enemy that is lurking around the corner, trying to creep in
while you are unaware. You let your guard down, and the enemy
slips between the cracks, and without you knowing it there he is,

riding in the same boat with you. You begin experiencing sin in a way that is only intended for the devil.

White-water rafting represents life, and the oars that are used to guide and stabilize the boat along with everything in it, including you, represent God's Holy Spirit. This is how subtle the enemy lures the innocent. Even though God's Holy Spirit issues a warning, everything looks so beautiful. That is how the enemy portrays sin. His job is "to steal, kill, and destroy" (John 10:10 NKJV). He is out to destroy the innocent.

God does not want us to be ignorant concerning the wiles of the devil. We are to be clearheaded and watchful; we are to be humble while "casting all of our care upon Him, for He cares for us" (1 Peter 5: 7 NKJV). God is able to keep us from falling (Jude 1:24). Although if we do fall into temptation, God is merciful. To God belongs the glory—for His grace!

> If my people who are called by My name will humble themselves, and pray and seek My face, and turn from their wicked ways, then I will hear from heaven, and will forgive their sin … (11 Chronicles 7:14).

Without God in our lives, we are like a ship without a sail or a rowboat without oars. Thanks, be unto God. He causes us to triumph through Christ Jesus. He is our way maker, and we must put our trust in Him.

Just as Abigail ran to God in times of despair, I also run to God. God is my secret place, my shelter from the storm. God is my rock, my strong tower, and my hiding place. God's arms gently cradle me. He is my comforter. God is my counselor when I am in need of advice. God is my way maker when I don't know which way to turn. God is my shining light when my way seems so dark. God is my friend when I'm alone. God is my encourager when I'm feeling down. God is my discerner when I don't know who to trust.

God is my peace giver when my soul feels anxious. Without God, I am nothing. I yearn for God's presence.

> I draw near to Him and He draws near to me.
> (James 4:8)

I turn to Him in prayer: Father, protect me with your knowledge that I may know and do Your will. Cover me with your righteousness that, through love, I will not sin against you. Reveal the truth to me so that I may live as Christ. Father, favor me with Your peace that I may take your good news to others. Increase my faith to know that You are surrounding me with Your keeping power. Cover me with your blood so that I may be used by the power of Your Holy Spirit wherever, whenever, and with whomever You choose. In Jesus's name I pray. Amen.

When a woman is devoted to God, she wants her character to resemble His. God molds her and shapes her into His likeness.

> Let us make man in our image, after our likeness.
> (Genesis 1:26 KJV)

This molding is sometimes a painful process, but it is a necessary procedure. Developing godly character is a habitual response to challenges, trials, and difficulties of life. Godly habits become godly character; and godly character becomes who we are. Abigail's response to David revealed her godly character. Her light was shown through her good works toward David, and God was glorified. She didn't have to try to fake it or try to be someone she was not.

Godly character is developed when we habitually allow God to handle the difficulties in our lives. Sometimes Christians are like a man walking down a road with a heavy bundle on his shoulders. He accepts a ride from a passing vehicle, yet after being seated, he refuses to remove the heavy bundle from his shoulders. He thinks that it would be asking too much of the driver to also carry his burden. Doesn't it sound silly to carry a heavy bundle on your shoulder while riding in a vehicle? Isn't that what we do when we hold on to our burdens rather than giving them to God.

Allowing God to carry our burdens over and over again is how we learn to trust in God. God tells us to cast all our cares upon Him because He cares for us. When casting my cares upon the Lord, I literally picture myself carrying my burden to the feet of Jesus and laying it down. Although, in developing godly character, we must carry our burdens to the Lord and learn to leave our burdens with Him. When we take our burdens to the Lord, we must not pick them up and bring them back with us. Leaving our burdens with the Lord is how we learn to totally trust God. When we trust God with our burdens, He will carry us in the midst of our trials.

The darkest time of my life was when God told me to go right and I went left. I walked away from God. Disobedience toward God makes Him appear a thousand miles away. We wonder where God is when we need Him the most. Although I left God, He never left me. I came to find out that during that dark time, He was carrying me when I couldn't carry myself. He created us, and He knows our frailties that we are but dust.

> I will never leave you nor forsake you. (Hebrews 13:5 NKJV)

God never leaves us alone. No matter how dark the trial may be, God is there with us. Trials come to make us strong. God wants us to stand strong in the midst of trials while He carries us in every situation.

In times of trials I have felt discouraged. I thought I was not passing the test. I came to realize that it wasn't about how well I thought I was doing. God was teaching me that His strength is made perfect in my weakness.

If we are to develop godly character, we cannot run from our situations. We grow in the dark times of life. Just as a child grows at night, we grow spiritually. During the dark hours of life—when things are not going as planned and trials and tribulations cross our paths—we are given an opportunity to learn to trust God with our situations. We watch Him work things out for our good.

Abigail displayed a godly character while standing as a strong woman of God. He carried her in the midst of her trial. During the dark times in our lives, we learn to trust God. Godly character is developed as we are drawn to His light that shines in our dark world, and we become more and more devoted—in love—with God.

CHAPTER 7

Understanding Concern for Others

We want revival in our cities, but we don't want to hear
anyone tell us that revival only comes when people are
hungry, when "vicarious intercessors" repent for sins they
never committed on behalf of people they've never met.
—Tommy Tenney, *The God Chasers*

To devotion to God, add concern for others.

> For I could wish that I myself were accursed from
> Christ for my brethren, my kinsmen according to
> the flesh. (Romans 9:3 KJV)

Abigail rode out to meet David, not knowing whether or not her
own life would be spared. She arose for the cause and stood in the
gap for others. Esther also stood in the gap for her people.

> Go, gather together all the Jews that are present
> in Shushan, and fast for me; neither eat nor drink
> for three days, night or day. My maids and I will
> fast likewise. And so I will go to the king, which

is against the law; and if I perish, I perish. (Esther
4:16 NKJV)

Through Esthers' devotion to her people, God spared her life—
and the lives of all the other Jews. The greatest sacrifice of all is
when Jesus laid down his life, so that we may live.

> While we were yet sinners, Christ died for us.
> (Romans 5:8 KJV)

Jesus laid down His life for His friends. What a marvelous thing
He did. He died so that we could live.

What are we willing to do for our brothers and sisters? How
concerned are we for one another? Do we show true concern for
one another?

> A certain man went down from Jerusalem to
> Jericho, and fell among thieves, who stripped
> him of his clothing, wounded him, and departed,
> leaving him half dead. Now a certain Samaritan,
> as he journeyed, came where he was. And when
> he saw him, he had compassion. So he went to
> him and bandaged his wounds, pouring on oil
> and wine; and he set him on his animal. On the
> next day, when he departed, he took out two
> denarii, gave them to the innkeeper, and said to
> him, "Take care of him; and whatever more you
> spend, when I come again, I will repay you." (Luke
> 10:30–35 NKJV)

How willing are we to help a brother or sister in need?

Assuredly, I say to you, in as much as you did it to
one of the least of these my brethren, you did it to
me. (Matthew 25:40 NKJV)

Showing concern for others is becoming Christ's hands and feet.
Love is God in action.

I recall a time when I had just gotten off of work. I looked both
ways before crossing the street. There was no traffic coming either
way, so I continued toward my car. As I reached the driver's side,
a man appeared on the other side of the car. He asked if I had any
money for a hot meal. Since the man had suddenly come out of
nowhere, I began to tremble with fear. Although I was trembling,
my heart's desire was to help the man since he appeared genuine
in his request. Fear seemed to be blocking my goodwill. My hands
were shaking so badly. I felt as though I was moving in slow
motion.

Through my slothfulness, the man began to walk away. I
cried, "Lord, I was going to help him." At that moment, my spirit
said, "And the fearful shall be cast into the lake of fire" (Revelation
21:8). God was trying to tell me that I could not help anyone by
being afraid. I had to get over my fear.

After I was held up at gunpoint, I became extremely fearful.
God knew I had to get over that fear. I took that fear to the feet of
Jesus and left it there. I don't recall when my fear actually left, but
at some point, fear was no longer dominating me.

Showing love takes courage. There will be times when we are
called to come out of our comfort zones to help others. Abigail
was called to confront a man with murder on his mind. At times
like those, we must rely on God to give us the strength we need
to be His servants, His hands, and His feet. God shows His love
through us. We must be willing to be vessels to be used by God.

> Be kindly affectionate to one another with brotherly love, in honor giving preference to one another. (Romans 12:10 NKJV)

In the United States, the land of plenty, we have so much. How willingly do we share? Nabal was rich and had more than enough, but through selfishness, he was unwilling to share of his substance. He was just like the rich fool that Jesus spoke about in Luke 12:16–21. The rich man's substance was so plentiful that he ran out of storage space. To solve the problem, he decided to build an enormous barn. The huge barn would allow him to retire, take it easy, eat, drink, and be merry. That night, after making this decision, the rich man died. Tomorrow is not promised to anyone; therefore, only what we do for others will last.

Charles R. Swindoll wrote about Gandhi in *The Tale of the Tardy Oxcart*.

> As Gandhi stepped aboard a train one day, one of his shoes slipped off and landed on the track. He was unable to retrieve it as the train was moving. To the amazement of his companions, Gandhi calmly took off his other shoe and threw it back along the track to land close to the first. Asked by a fellow passenger why he did so, Gandhi smiled. "The poor man who finds the shoe lying on the track," he replied, "will now have a pair he can use."

> My little children let us not love in word, or in tongue; but in deed and in truth. (1 John 3:18 NKJV)

It is said that people do not care how much we know, until they know how much we care.

> We are the light of the world ... let our light shine
> before men, that they may see our good works
> and glorify our Father in heaven. (Matthew 5:14–
> 16 KJV)

When we do good works, we exemplify Christ for the world to see. Nabal wanted his status to be made known, but David and his men weren't concerned about how important Nabal thought he was. David just wanted Nabal to treat his men with the same respect they had treated Nabal's men with.

Abigail presented a true concern for others. She did not question her actions toward David. She treated him as she would have wanted to be treated. Abigail thought more highly of others than she did herself. When we possess this same sort of mentality, we will live unselfishly. We will not have a problem when it comes to sharing our substance or kindness. We will be givers and not takers. We will be lenders and not borrowers. A good woman will show favor and lend (Psalm 112:5). She will think of giving as an opportunity to serve the Lord. She will say, "Bless the Lord," and she will not always say, "Lord, bless me." Jesus said that the second greatest command is "You shall love your neighbor as yourself" (Matthew 22:39 NKJV).

The law of kindness was upon Abigail's tongue. When she spoke to David, her words were gentle words of blessings.

> The Lord will always protect you and your family,
> because you fight for him. I pray that you won't
> ever do anything evil as long as you live. The Lord
> your God will keep you safe when enemies try
> to kill you. But he will snatch away their lives
> quicker than you can throw a rock from a sling.
> The Lord has promised to do many good things
> for you, even to make you the ruler of Israel. The
> Lord will keep his promises to you, and now

your conscience will be clear, because you won't
be guilty of taking revenge and killing innocent
people. When the Lord does all those good things
for you, please remember me. (1 Samuel 25:28–31)

A soft answer turns away wrath, but a harsh word stirs up anger
(Proverbs 15:1 NKJV). Words should be like a gift: wrapped in
beautiful paper with a stunning bow on top. When someone
presents me a gift, and I notice that person has meticulously taken
the time to wrap it so beautifully—no matter what is in the box, or
whether the person has spent thousands of dollars or less than a
dollar—I feel that that person's heart was in the giving. He or she
gave with only the best intentions. If our words were given that
way, they would always bless and not curse.

Through faith, Abigail saw the mountain that stood before
her. She spoke blessings into David's life, but she didn't end with
those words. She went on to speak blessings into her own life as
well. Abigail asked David to remember her when the Lord did all
those good things that she spoke about. We can use our tongues
to bless our lives and the lives of others—or we can use the same
tongues to curse our lives and the lives of those we speak to.

We bless others as we serve them with kindness. Jesus came
to serve and not to be served. Those in higher positions are
the greater servants. Whoever wants to be first must be a slave
for all. How would your family or my family react if we were
to come home and brag to them that we had been chosen as a
slave? I would expect that not much excitement would be shown.
Enslavement is not what Jesus meant when He said that He came
to serve and not to be served. A servant's job is to do all he or she
can to make life better for others—to free them to be everything
they can be. A servant's first interest is others. Servanthood is a
loving choice we make to minister to others. It is not a result of
coercion or manipulation, which we can easily fall prey to unless

we understand the underlying dynamics and how the nature of Jesus prevents it.

The chief means of resisting manipulation is humility—knowing who we really are and facing it. Through humbleness, hostility is overshadowed by gentleness and undermined by self-control. Although David was angry, Abigail chose to humble herself and not become a victim of hostility.

> Therefore, humble yourselves under the mighty
> hand of God, that He may exalt you in due time.
> (1 Peter 5:6 NKJV)

Abigail could have become angry with Nabal for putting her in a situation where she had to humbly apologize for an act she did not commit. Instead, Abigail humbly gave up her right to hurt back—and that is forgiveness.

When we forgive others, we open the doors to our hearts that allow mercy and grace to come in. By forgiving, we are forgiven. Abigail's true concern for others did not leave room for unforgiveness. It was a God-given action—based upon love.

In our genuine concern for others, the world may view our strength as weakness and try to take advantage of our kindness. Therefore, God gives us a spirit of discernment to know the intents of the heart. Discernment is similar to someone's eyes adjusting to the dark: we can see the enemy coming, but the enemy can't see us. God does not want us to be ignorant of the devil's devices that are used to take advantage of us. God wants us to be free to be the light of the world so that we may freely show concern for one another.

"For greater is He that is in you than he that is in the world" (1 John 4:4 KJV). When we have God living inside us—no matter how the world treats us—we can show concern and keep going. When people treat us in illogical or unreasonable ways, we can forgive them and keep going. When we are treated with unkindness because of God who lives in us, we can show kindness to the unkindly and keep going. When God tells us to do something for others—even if they don't appreciate it—we can keep going. People may reject us for doing good, but we must remember that they are rejecting God and not us. When we have God living in us, we have no excuse for not showing concern for others.

God is no respecter of persons. He makes the sun to shine on the just and the unjust. Therefore, we are never exempt from showing concern for others.

CHAPTER 8

Understanding Love

To concern for others, add love.

> Owe no one anything, except to love one another:
> for he who loves another has fulfilled the law.
> For the commandments, "You shall not commit
> adultery," "You shall not murder," "You shall
> not steal," "You shall not bear false witness,"
> "You shall not covet," and if there is any other
> commandment, are all summed up in this saying,
> namely, "You shall love your neighbor as yourself."
> Love does no harm to a neighbor; therefore love
> is the fulfillment of the law. (Romans 13:8–10
> NKJV)

They shall know that we are Christians by our love. Love is demonstrated from one heart to another. Love is charity (1 Corinthians 13 KJV). When love is a verb, it is an action. Therefore, charity means love in action. Does the world know us by our love?

Abigail understood that her job was to love her husband—and that it was God's job to make him good. Abigail understood the mechanism of loving a difficult person like Nabal. In her wisdom, she understood that, when we feel that we can't, God says, "I can." When the task of loving someone becomes too hard, all we have to do is ask God to love that person through us.

> You have not because you ask not. (James 4:2b NKJV)

The only excuse people have for not loving others is not wanting to. God is love, and if we ask God to love someone through us, He will. When we allow God to love a person through us, we learn to let go and let God.

When we decide to let go and let God, we are choosing to no longer enable others. We allow others to learn from natural consequences. We will not be in denial of certain situations. We accept things for what they are, knowing that God is able to turn things around. When we allow God to take over, we permit others to face up to reality instead of trying to protect them. We stop trying to fix people, but we are there to support them. Instead of fear, love is personified when we allow God to take over.

God loves us and gives us free will. Love does not demand that someone meet our expectations. Love is allowing others the freedom to be who they are. By freeing others, we become free to love. True love is not selfish. It does not demand its own way. Love is freely given and must be freely received.

> As I have loved you, love one another. (John 13:34)

We are to imitate Christ's love for us. Jesus did not wait until we were lovely to love us. He did not wait to be asked. Jesus loved first. When we imitate Christ's love, we say, "Even if you never change, this is what God would have me do for you. Even if you never repay me, this is how God wants me to love you."

Through Abigail's actions, she was saying, "Nabal, even if you never change, this is how God wants me to love you." Her actions toward David showed that she could not close her heart to a need that God had given her the ability to meet. Even if David never repaid her, that was how God wanted her to show love.

What need has God given us the ability to meet? Perhaps there is a neighbor we haven't seen lately. We know in our hearts that a visit is long overdue. Maybe we have missed seeing someone at church for the past few weeks. A call may be an answer to someone's prayer if he or she has been feeling as though no one cares or is concerned. We can do all the thinking about a person that we want to, but if we do not actually make an effort to call or reach out to people to let them know that we truly care, they will never know. Sometimes a small acknowledgement is all that is needed to make people know they are missed and loved.

Nabal was not always as kind to Abigail as he should have been. What do we do when God call us to meet a need for someone who has misused us or treated us unkindly? God is not asking us to be doormats. He asks us to show loving kindness. As Christians, we are to be bold as lions and as meek as lambs. It takes a bigger person to speak words of kindness when there is hostile tension in the air.

When we love like Christ, we cannot hold onto bitterness, resentment, or hostility and expect to have a good relationship with God.

> If someone says, "I love God" and hates his brother, he is a liar; for he who does not love his brother whom he has seen, how can he love God whom he has not seen. (1 John 4:20 NKJV)

God never tells us that we are to show love only when someone treats us kindly. God tells us to do unto others as we would have others do unto us.

But if you love those who love you, what credit is
that to you? For even sinners love those who love
them. And if you do good to those who do good
to you, what credit is that to you? For even sinners
do the same. (Luke 6:32–33 NKJV)

Sometimes the thing God asks us to do is not easy. God may ask
us to show love for others at a time when we feel that our very
own hearts are about to break. God asks us to love unselfishly. He
wants us to put the needs of others before our own needs.

Love your enemies, do good, and you will be sons
and daughters of the Most High. (Luke 6:35)

Unselfish love caused Jesus—who knew no sin—to take on our
sins. When unselfish love becomes visible, non-Christians ask,
"How can you love like that?"

Abigail publicly exposed an unselfish love when she set out
to meet David on his way to kill her family. Thinking more
highly of others than herself, she took Nabal's guilt upon herself
and apologized for her foolish husband. She wanted David to
understand and realize that she knew nothing of the matter. She
did not harp upon Nabal's foolishness. She merely stated the facts
and left it alone. Abigail had not committed the offense. She was
not present during the insult. She asked David to forgive her. How
could Abigail take on Nabal's sin? In order for Abigail to ask David
to forgive her for an offense she did not commit, she had to give
the transgression to God. God tells us to cast our cares upon Him
because He cares for us.

When I give my cares to God, I picture myself kneeling at the
feet of Jesus and laying whatever care I have at His feet. I realize
that I must not go back to the feet of Jesus and pick up that care. I
must leave that care there. James 1:7–8 tells us that double-minded
people are unstable in all their ways and will receive nothing from

the Lord. I trust God with all of my cares because He loves me. I know that He is able to handle them. Abigail could ask David to forgive her for Nabal's sin because of God's perfect and amazing love. God loves us so much that He gave His only Son—who knew no sin—to become sin for us. God's love for us is truly amazing!

Love for the Lord accomplishes what fear of the law could never achieve.

> He that has my commandments, and keeps them,
> it is he who loves me. (John 14:21 KJV)

We keep the commandments because they are commandments of the Lord. When we truly love God, we want to obey Him. We want His will—and not our will—to be done in our lives so that God will be glorified.

> A good understanding have all those who do His
> commandments. (Psalm 111:10 NKJV)

If we want to have good understanding, we must obey God. Through obedience, we will be blessed. Blessed are those who delight in obeying God (Psalm 112:1). Abigail obeyed God by being tenderhearted and humble. She didn't repay evil for evil. She did not retaliate with insults; on the contrary, she returned blessings. She knew that she was called to inherit a blessing.

> If you want to enjoy life and see many happy days,
> keep your tongue from speaking evil and your
> lips form telling lies. Turn away from evil and
> do good. Search for peace, and work to maintain
> it. The eyes of the Lord watch over those who do
> right, and His ears are open to their prayers. But
> the Lord turns His face against those who do evil.
> (1 Peter 3:10–12 NLT)

Through Abigail's obedience unto the Lord, she was blessed. She became the wife of King David.

> And David sent and proposed to Abigail, to take her as his wife. Then she arose, bowed her face to the earth, and said, "Here is your maidservant, a servant to wash the feet of the servants of my lord." So Abigail rose in haste and rode on a donkey, attended by five of her maidens; and she followed the messengers of David, and became his wife. (1 Samuel 25:39b–42 NKJV)

Love shows the world that we are Christians; yet sadly, the world also knows whether or not our love is real. We must follow the way of love.

> Though I speak with the tongues of men and of angels, but have not love, I have become as sounding brass, or a clanging cymbal. And though I have the gift of prophecy, and understand all mysteries and all knowledge, and though I have all faith, so that I could remove mountains, but have not love, I am nothing. And though I bestow all my goods to feed the poor, and though I give my body to be burned, but have not love, it profits me nothing. Love suffers long and is kind; love does not envy; love does not parade itself, is not puffed up; does not behave rudely, does not seek its own, is not provoked, thinks no evil; does not rejoice in iniquity, but rejoices in the truth; bears all things, believes all things, hopes all things, endures all things. Love never fails. But whether there are prophecies, they will fail; whether there are tongues, they will cease; whether there

is knowledge, it will vanish away. For we know in part and we prophesy in part. But when that which is perfect has come, then that which is in part will be done away. When I was a child, I spoke as a child, I understood as a child, I thought as a child; but when I became a man, I put away childish things. For now we see in a mirror, dimly, but then face to face. Now I know in part, but then I shall know just as I also am known. And now abide faith, hope, love, these three, but the greatest of these is love. (1 Corinthians 13 NKJV)

Abigail's love was real, and its genuineness was displayed through her actions. What does love look like? Love has hands to help, feet to rush to the poor and needy, eyes to see misery and want, and ears to hear the sighs and sorrows of men. Love is something that every human heart cries for. The New Testament describes four kinds of love:

- *stergo* (natural affection): the love we have for our families
- *eros* (self-serving passion): love for the sole purpose of sexual satisfaction
- *phileo* (friendship): love for one with whom his or her company is enjoyed
- *agape* (giving of one's self): totally selfless love that comes from and is rooted in God

Love is the giving of oneself to another. It's a skill that is developed in the strength of God's Spirit.

Love your enemies, bless those who curse you, do good to those who hate you, and pray for those who spitefully use you and persecute you. (Matthew 5:44 NKJV)

Love insists that we do something. Abigail's love spoke through her actions.

Every act of kindness—even a small one—can make a difference. Sharing a smile, a look of affirmation, or a short but sincere compliment can make another person's day turn from sadness to joy. Do not overlook the importance of good manners and generosity. Opening a door or yielding to another car in traffic can influence someone's life in a positive way.

When we walk close to God, we come to realize that we could never surpass God's love. Love is who God is.

> Love each other. Just as I have loved you, you
> should love each other. Your love for one another
> will prove to the world that you are my disciples.
> (John 13:34–35 NLT)

We love one another as Christ loved the church and gave Himself for it. Through the giving of Himself, Christ exemplified His love for us. Our love for others is revealed through giving. Giving is not just monetary—it is shown through actions of kindness, deeds, and words spoken. Abigail's love was shown as she gave in deed and words.

One way to show our love for God is by being grateful for all things. As we observe nature, we see God through the ruffling of leaves as He gently blows His breath upon them. God tells us that He loves us through flowers and scenic views that take our breath away. There are times—even though it may not be intentional—that we take God's love for granted. God paints a beautiful rainbow in the sky, and we don't even notice. When we are working in the hot sun and God sends a gentle breeze to fan us, we don't show gratitude. When God prevents a collision, we don't say thank you. When a child goes to bed with a fever and wakes up feeling cool, we don't thank the Lord. When a child is not hungry when he goes to bed, we don't thank the Lord. How we must grieve God's heart when He knows that we take His love for granted.

God says that He will never leave us or forsake us. He will always be with us. He patiently waits for us to talk to Him and spend time with Him. At times, we ignore Him. Wouldn't it sadden our hearts to have a friend ignore us? How must God feel when we ignore Him? Is God the center of our thoughts?

Love is a choice, and because of God's love for us, He gives us the freedom to choose to love Him and everyone else. True love is not a forced behavior. It is freedom.

Out of all of the gifts God gives us, the greatest gift is love. God gives us the freedom to love all of humanity. We are free to show love and empathy toward the hurting and compassion to those less fortunate than ourselves. We are free to forgive those who have trespassed against us. Love covers a multitude of sins.

When Abigail approached David with a loving heart of compassion, David's thoughts were no longer on Nabal's rude and bitter words. His focus was on Abigail's love and kindness. When others see us, let them see hearts of love—and let our actions be reflections of God.

God is love, and because God is omnipresent, we are able to find love in everything. Love is found in the songs that birds sing, in the flowers that bloom, in babies' faces, and in smiles that brighten someone's day. We do not have to look very far to find love.

> Behold, I stand at the door and knock: if any man
> hear my voice, and open the door, I will come in
> to him, and will sup with him, and he with me.
> (Revelation 3:20 KJV)

All we have to do is open our hearts and allow God's love to come in—that is the true pathway to understanding.

Bibliography

Contemporary English Version (CEV) Bible. American Bible Society, n. d.

English Standard Version (ESV) Bible, YouVersion.com.

Good News Translation (GNT) Bible, YouVersion.com.

King James Version (KJV) Bible. American Bible Society, n. d.

New King James Version (NKJV) Bible, Thomas Nelson Inc., 1982.

New Living Testament (NLT) Bible, YouVersion.com.

Swindoll, Charles R. *The Tale of the Tardy Oxcart*, Nashville: Word Publishing, 1998.

Tenney, Tommy. *The God Chasers*, Shippensburg: Reproduced by permission of Destiny Image ® Publishers, Inc., 1998.

About the Author

Yonnie Fowler was born in Jackson, Michigan, where she still resides with her husband Billy whom she married in 1971. They have one son and two daughters and are enjoying the addition to the family of grandchildren. She attends Second Missionary Baptist Church, and is a graduate of Covington Theological Seminary.

Printed in the United States
By Bookmasters